The Flower Garden
Coloring Book

Ruth Soffer

Dover Publications, Inc.
Mineola, New York

Publisher's Note

Tending a garden can be a relaxing and rewarding experience as you watch the fruits of your labor grow and blossom into a breathtaking display. While a typical one may generally consist of a few shrubs, some trees, and a splash of flowers, a "specialized" garden reflects the gardener's individual taste and needs, and can provide a welcome sanctuary from the stresses of the day.

There are many different types of gardens to choose from. You can, for example, group together flowers for a seasonal showcase of color, or have a garden that will attract butterflies to your yard. If you live near a pond, you can create a gorgeous array with plants that thrive in water or moist soil. And for those who have limited space available, you can enjoy a container garden in your home, on a patio, or on a terrace.

Out of the thirty spectacular gardens selected for this coloring book, you are sure to find one that will inspire you to start a garden of your own. Under each illustration you will find a description of the type of garden, along with the common and scientific names of the plants used to create these masterpieces from nature.

Bibliographical Note

The Flower Garden Coloring Book is a new work, first published by Dover Publications, Inc., in 2005.

International Standard Book Number

ISBN-13: 978-0-486-44497-0
ISBN-10: 0-486-44497-X

Manufactured in the United States by RR Donnelley
44497X08   2015
www.doverpublications.com

An Autumn Garden
Virginia Creeper *(Parthenocissus quinquefolia)*, Firethorn *(Pyracantha* sp.), White-crowned Sparrow.

An Early Fall Garden
Pumpkin (Cucurbitaceae family), Sunflower (*Helianthus* sp.).

A Cascading Garden
Chinese Wisteria *(Wisteria sinensis)*, Scarlet Hawthorn (Rosaceae family).

3

A Vegetable Garden

Tomato (Solanaceae family), Squash (Cucurbitaceae family).

A Shaded Foliage Garden

Hosta (*Hosta* sp.).

A Succulent Garden

FRONT LEFT: (*Cotyledon luteosquamata*), FRONT RIGHT: (*Sedum* sp.),
BACKGROUND: Hens and Chicks (*Sempervivum* sp.) and (*Echeveria* sp.)—all from the Crassulaceae family.

A Pond Garden

Caladium (Araceae family), Hardy Water Canna *(Thalia dealbata)*, Water Lily *(Nymphaea* sp.).

A Rock Garden

Cosmos *(Cosmos bipinnatus)*, Snapdragon *(Antirrhinum majus)*,
Campanula *(Campanula garganica)*, Monarch Butterfly.

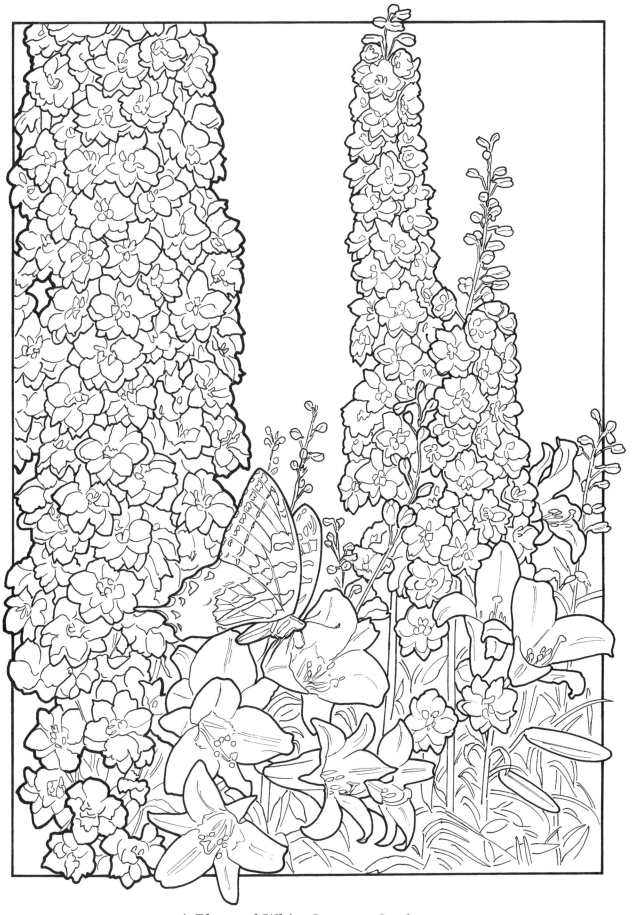

A Blue and White Summer Garden

Larkspur (*Delphinium* sp.), Regal Lily *(Lilium regale)*, Tiger Swallowtail Butterfly.

A Climbing Garden
Clematis (Ranunculaceae family).

A Suburban Garden
Gladiola (*Gladiolus* sp.), Petunia (*Petunia x hybrida*).

A Butterfly Garden
Red Violets (*Viola* sp.), Butterfly Weed *(Asclepias tuberosa)*, Fritillary Butterflies.

A Garden Overflowing with Color
Oriental Poppy (*Papaver orientale*), Lupine (*Lupinus polyphyllus*), Deer Fawn.

A Rose Garden

(*Rosa* sp.) from the Rosaceae family.

A Summer Garden in Full Bloom

FOREGROUND: Marigold (*Tagetes* sp.), Petunia (*Petunia x hybrida*),
WATERING CAN: Larkspur (*Delphinium* sp.), African Daisy (*Gerbera jamesonii*), Zinnia (*Zinnia elegans*).

20

A Spring Bulb Garden
Tulips *(Tulipa Gesneriana)*, Daffodil *(Narcissus* sp.).

A Fragrant Garden

Sweet Pea *(Lathyrus odoratus)*, Snapdragon *(Antirrhinum majus)*, Cornflower *(Centaurea cyanus)*, Elder Flower *(Sambucus nigra)*.

A Cactus Garden

BOTTOM RIGHT: *(Matucana madisoniorum)*, BOTTOM LEFT: *(Mammillaria saboae)*,
CENTER RIGHT: *(Astrophytum ornatum)*, CENTER: Crown Cactus *(Rebutia* sp.),
TOP RIGHT: Monk's Hood *(Astrophytum ornatum)*, TOP LEFT: Teddy Bear Cholla *(Opuntia bigelovi).*

A Pastel Late Summer Garden
Rock Rose (Cistaceae family), Pink Hydrangea (Hydrangeaceae family),
Green Santolina *(Santolina virens)*, *(Senecio* sp.) from the Compositae family.

A Winter Garden

Lenten Rose (*Helleborus orientalis*), Snowdrop (*Galanthus nivalis*), White-throated Sparrow.

An Edible Flower Garden
Marigold *(Calendula officinalis)*, Nasturtium/Double Nasturtium *(Tropaeolum majus)*,
Borage *(Borago officinalis)*, Elder Flower *(Sambucus nigra)*.

An Arrangement of Garden Flowers

Lenten Rose *(Helleborus orientalis)*, Cherry Tree Blossoms (*Prunus* sp.), Ivy (*Hedera* sp.),
(*Mahonia* sp.) from the Berberidaceae family, Tulips *(Tulipa Gesneriana)*,
Polyanthus (Primulaceae family), Forsythia (*Forsythia* sp.).